See You On the Other Side of Through

See You On the Other Side of Through

Pepper E. Totten *and* Timothy K. Totten

Copyright © 2016 Pepper E. Totten and Timothy K. Totten.

All rights reserved. No part of this book may be used or reproduced by any means, graphic, electronic, or mechanical, including photocopying, recording, taping or by any information storage retrieval system without the written permission of the author except in the case of brief quotations embodied in critical articles and reviews.

Scripture taken from the King James Version of the Bible.

Scripture taken from the Holy Bible, NEW INTERNATIONAL VERSION®. Copyright © 1973, 1978, 1984, 2011 by Biblica, Inc. All rights reserved worldwide. Used by permission. NEW INTERNATIONAL VERSION® and NIV® are registered trademarks of Biblica, Inc. Use of either trademark for the offering of goods or services requires the prior written consent of Biblica US, Inc.

Archway Publishing books may be ordered
through booksellers or by contacting:

Archway Publishing
1663 Liberty Drive
Bloomington, IN 47403
www.archwaypublishing.com
1 (888) 242-5904

Because of the dynamic nature of the Internet, any web addresses or links contained in this book may have changed since publication and may no longer be valid. The views expressed in this work are solely those of the author and do not necessarily reflect the views of the publisher, and the publisher hereby disclaims any responsibility for them.

Any people depicted in stock imagery provided by Thinkstock are models, and such images are being used for illustrative purposes only. Certain stock imagery © Thinkstock.

ISBN: 978-1-4808-2915-2 (sc)
ISBN: 978-1-4808-2917-6 (e)

Library of Congress Control Number: 2016904178

Print information available on the last page.

Archway Publishing rev. date: 5/4/2016

Check Your Mail

Though I walk in the midst of trouble, thou wilt receive me: thou shalt stretch forth thine hand against the wrath of mine enemies, and thy right hand shall save me.

Psalm 138:7 KJV

All people—whether rich, poor, or somewhere in the middle—go through hard times. The difference between what you go through and what the next person might be faced with is how you choose to play the hand you're dealt. For example, the more you play a sport, an instrument, or a card game, the better you become at overtaking any opponent. The same is true for life situations. The more things you overcome, the better prepared you become for future trials.

Amid his 2014 comedy tour, Bill Cosby, America's favorite dad from the highly acclaimed *The Cosby Show,* found himself the subject of an evolving sex scandal that promised to change his life forever. One woman after another reported to the media surprisingly similar stories of how Cosby used his power and celebrity status to commit heinous sexual assaults. Accusers, some teary-eyed and others with expressions of bitter anger, told tales of one-night incidents with Cosby that reportedly occurred twenty, thirty, forty, and even fifty years ago. The women could not recall details of the personal attacks, indicating that Cosby obviously slipped a drug into their drinks before the alleged rape. Cosby denied the charges.

Why now? Why at the age of seventy-seven was Bill Cosby being accused? If these crimes did happen, why did the women not speak out before now? As social media and the nightly news reported the growing accusations of drugged drinks and rape, the women's stories—with no evidence, no witnesses, and no apparent validity—became more ridiculous day by day. Because the statute of limitations had expired, prohibiting legal procedures or ramifications, the women had nothing to gain other than bragging rights for tainting the reputation of a well-respected man and entertainer. On the other hand, professionally, Cosby had everything to lose. He could be guilty and then again, he could be innocent. The public may never know what really happened between Cosby and his accusers mainly because there are generally three versions to any story—his version, the others' version, and God's truth.

Life often seems like the world's largest roller-coaster ride. It leaves us gasping for air, dazed and clinching anything or anyone who might deliver us from sudden downfalls, lightning-speed curves, and hoops that leave our insides in a topsy-turvy mess. We may find ourselves searching for stability from a flood of unexpected dips and astonishing directional changes that cause us to lose our way and give rise to questions of how to cope and what path to take for some sense of stability. There is hope even in times of confusion and bewilderment. The answers we look for are often within reach and in plain view. They may be so close that if they were wrapped in the body of a venomous snake, you and I would have been bitten a long time ago.

Even when we are at our lowest points, life has a strange way of providing what's needed at the most critical time. For example, after the court commander heard of the plot to assassinate the apostle Paul, he quickly sent Paul to Caesarea with a letter explaining his innocence to the governor, Felix (Acts 23:16–35 KJV). A few words on a sheet of paper changed the direction of Paul's life. It was not about what he knew but who he knew. While education serves as a vehicle to get from one destination to the next, the right connections are like bulletproof wheels to ensure a quick and safe arrival. While it is possible to travel in a vehicle without wheels, it is better to have at least four. A simple piece of mail written by the right person was delivered at a most crucial time to save Paul's life. Had Paul not checked and opened his mail, his outcome would have been vastly different.

When was the last time you checked your mail? Yes, mail. There are two types of mail—junk mail and personal mail. Mail is something sent to you, often for your eyes only. It has your name on it. It was created with you and your needs in mind. However, we must approach cautiously because distributors of junk mail are well educated in conning unsuspecting people. These con artists send information deceptively by mail, phone, and social media.

In order to stop the momentum of attacks by crooks, life must be approached carefully and thoughtfully, especially when going through a storm. At one point in my life I had no job, bills were piling up, and my child needed school supplies. As part of my usual routine, at 3p.m., I walked down the driveway to check the mailbox. Grocery ads and other sale papers were wrapped around a bundle of letters that had been carefully placed inside my mailbox. My first thought was to drop the entire bundle into the garbage can. I didn't need to see any misleading advertisements or to collect any more trash. *Why rush?* I thought, *I have nothing else to do. But I can at least look at it.* So without opening any of the pieces, I quickly glanced at each letter before dropping them into the garbage can. The last two pieces were from my car insurance company. Like all previous letters, they were also dropped into the garbage. As soon as these letters landed, I heard a voice whisper, "At least see what they have to say." Much to my surprise, the first one had a $500 check for not having insurance claims. The other explained the future arrival of the $500 check. Glory to God! Now my child could go on that field trip with her class, and I could get some personal things we need. In order to get this blessing, I had to literally check my mail. That blessing received was almost a blessing missed.

Countless times during counseling sessions, clients have talked to us about missed opportunities due to fear. This fear stemmed from fear of failure, and many times there was also an unrelenting fear of success. When applying for a promotion, there is the expectation of added responsibility. Some fear they will actually be granted the promotion and then develop a sense of inadequacy when the realization of added responsibility sets in. Others, knowing they were the most qualified, still failed to apply for a position. But they became apprehensive due to the fear they would no longer be able to maintain friendships with those within their current pay scale. They forget that the same God who answered the prayers for a promotion can also answer prayers for additional help and guidance in fulfilling new responsibilities.

Sometimes blessings come to us in simple ways, like through the mail, an unexpected delivery, or a routine trip to the grocery store. But many times the mail we need to check is simply our picking up the Word of God. I picked up the mail, but had I not opened the letter to read the message inside, I would have blocked my own blessing. You can pick up a job application, but if you never complete and submit it to the proper authorities, you will never know what could have been. How many times have you been on a job and wondered how Joe Blow got the job because he's uneducated, unsociable, and unqualified? That could be because qualified people such as you were paralyzed by fear and failed to apply.

How many times do I pick up the Bible or download a Bible app only to figuratively toss it into the proverbial garbage can? Although I originally counted my blessing found in the mail as rubbish, I repented when I returned to retrieve it. It was for me. The Word of God is for me, too. One of my favorite books is the book of Proverbs. This book provides instruction on how to live my life. In order to make it more personal, I simply insert my name in the Scripture. This is a way to see that a blessing delayed is not a blessing denied. You may have prayed and prayed for something with no word from the Lord. Start by giving God a portion of your time. The Bible teaches that we should give to God as well as to our fellow neighbors in order to receive great blessings. "Give, and it shall be given unto you; good measure, pressed down, and shaken together, and running over, shall men give unto your bosom. For with the same measure that ye mete withal it shall be measured to you again" (Luke 6:38 KJV).

Check your mail. God does not expect you to be perfect at the beginning of your journey; not even in the middle. His expectations are that we all be lifelong learners. Start by inserting your name in the Scriptures to make the Word of God more personal. Try by taking the initial step of inserting your name in the above Scripture. What are you willing to give? Who will you give to, and how often?

Delayed, but not Denied

For our light and momentary troubles are achieving for us an eternal glory that far outweighs them all.

2 Corinthians 4:17 NIV

One of the most difficult times in life is when a parent loses a child. Human nature, regardless of cultural background, understands the many challenges parents face in these tough situations. Depending on the circumstances of the child's death, prayer vigils are often organized, and dedicated friends and family support each other with love and compassion. Additionally, the newly bereaved parents receive an outpouring of love from the community as shown by beautiful floral arrangements, monetary contributions, food, and other gifts. These are acceptable responses.

Time and again, this outpouring of affection is not as prevalent in instances when the child dies prior to birth, such as a miscarriage or stillbirth. Because no baby came home with his or her parents, people have a tendency to minimize the physical and emotional pain associated with the loss. Not just those in the community at large, but family, friends, and fellow Christians often add to the pain. This is done by either acting as if nothing happened or by speaking hurtful words. Many well-meaning, kindhearted people tend to believe they are being sympathetic by saying the loss of life was, "a blessing from the Lord." Or it might be declared that "You are young and can try again later," or it is "just a flesh wound." In the midst of feeling the pain from the loss, it is difficult to see the blessing. Instead, the person delivering the message is seen as cruel and heartless.

In His infinite wisdom and understanding of human socialization, God created us with two ears and one mouth. Theoretically, this would inform people to listen twice as much as they speak. James, a servant of God, wrote, "Let every man be swift to hear, slow to speak, slow to wrath" (James 1:19 KJV). Unfortunately, many have failed at this basic task. In sympathizing with someone in their time of bereavement, it's important to put the ears to use more than the mouth. People, especially older females, can become dogmatic when talking with young unwed mothers. To avoid advancing the already present pain, listen to understand the feelings, desires, and thought patterns of the wounded. Listen without judging and without interruption.

During difficult times both men and women can benefit from talking the situation over with a trusted friend who is more interested in listening than offering advice. Poorly thought out words may cause a distressed person to lash out against well-meaning friends and family. Negative words could also cause the person to become angry with God. When experiencing a loss, those with noble intentions could actually turn the broken-hearted to turn against this god that thought it appropriate for them to experience pain or thought it good to take their precious child before she or he was given a chance at life. Instead of speaking without regards to the impact that words may have on the listener, allow all expressions to be filled with genuine love one for another (Ephesians 4:6 KJV; I Corinthians 13:4, 13 KJV; I Corinthians 16:14 KJV).

The following is an excerpt from Pepper's personal journal regarding her first of two experiences with miscarriages. Unlike the second occasion, only a handful of people knew of the first pregnancy.

> *4/25/2013*
> *So yesterday I finally went to the doctor. I am pregnant! What have I done? What seemed like a good idea (taking out the Nuvaring birth control) now seems like my worst mistake. I am not married. I am not engaged. I am alone. Yeah Tim is still around, but I just feel so all alone. I went to his place yesterday to tell him. He was speechless. He also refused to turn the TV off to talk to me. He would rather watch wrestling than discuss this big event for both of us. I just graduated with my doctorate. I'm looking for a job. I have no idea what Tim is doing. I just want to leave. I am scared. What do I do now? This is big. I will have to pay for all of this. I am paying for it financially, emotionally, psychologically,*

and physically. I have been trying to check in with Tim to see how he is doing with it, but he says nothing. NO ONE!!! No One checks on me. Not once has Tim asked me how I am doing.

Events that are significant for you may not be as important to others. Although I felt abandoned, I was not alone. God was right there walking beside me every step of the way. As small as it may seem to many people, God provided a listening ear and the pillow that dried my tears at night. When feeling pain, sometimes we can get a small level of comfort in little things, like a smile from a stranger or the soft touch of wind against a tear-stained face.

4/30/2013

What a whirlwind! Wednesday, I found out officially that I am pregnant. Friday, Tim and I went for an ultra-sound. The technicians said they see nothing. Matter of fact I was asked if I was sure I was pregnant. At 4:45am Saturday, I was cramping and in immense pain. I went to the bathroom to discover that I was bleeding. I called the Cigna insurance nurse for advice. She said I was spotting, but could wait till later in the morning to call the doctor. I called my doctor, but got the on-call doctor. I decided to wait it out. Not much more bleeding Saturday and none Sunday. Monday morning I was bleeding with what looked like blood clots. The cramps were severe; about a 9 on a 1-10 scale. I decided I would go to ER after taking Zhariah to school. I didn't tell Tim until about 7:20 am when I was on my way. I knew he couldn't take any time off work and I was going to put my big girl panties on and go to the hospital. I was the only person in the waiting room. I was dressed for work in a sheer pale-peach, yellowish long-sleeved button-up shirt, ankle length burgundy skirt, and flat brown shoes. The security guard walked by a few times and asked if I was with someone because surely I was not sick. I was there for 6 hours. They took blood and connected a needle to prep for an IV. I was then given a very painful internal ultrasound. The technician showed me the gestational sac and said the pregnancy was in my uterus where it belonged. I left the hospital at 2pm.

By the time Tim got to my house it was about 8:30pm. I passed the embryo; it was a relief from intense pain. My emotions were weird. It all was confusing. I felt relief from going through an unwanted pregnancy. I had relief that Tim was there with me. I still don't really know how I feel about everything. It all happened so fast. Here today, gone tomorrow—literally. I did not get a chance to bond with the baby. Now I have, *we have been given the opportunity to do things the right way, God's way.*

Keeping it moving. Right now I am on the bus to New York with Zhariah and her school choir. Maybe this will be a sort of healing trip for me. I have been under so much stress and pressure; I sometimes don't even recognize myself.

Pain, through its blinding nature, prevents understanding. All the body can focus on is how much it really hurts. Chances are, until the pain subsides, there is little thought given to what lessons can be learned or even how life can be better in the hereafter. Prayer, even a simple plea to God asking for relief, can be the beginning steps to healing. After her physical pain dwindled down, the blinders were removed and Pepper began to regain a sense of normality. Previously, when she wrote "I just want to leave," her deepest, darkest desire was to end her life. As a devout Christian, she knew this would lead to sure damnation, but the pain blinded her. Although she had not yet fully understood what happened or why it happened to her, after the storm of pain passed, Pepper was willing to pick up the pieces and move forward with her life.

<u>Tim's Point Of View:</u>

How do men really deal with miscarriages? This is one question that has handicapped the male population for many years. As men, we are not structured to be as verbal or as emotional as women in many cases. However, we do have an emotional side that very few women ever see.

When Pepper and I lost our first child to a miscarriage, it was just as hard for me as it was for her. Of course she wouldn't know this because my male ego wouldn't allow my emotions to surface. One of the main reasons it hurt me is because I had no children and had always wondered if I would ever have any. When I was first told by Pepper that she was pregnant, there was some hesitation on my part because due to my past, I had begun to think that I was unable to reproduce. I continued to feel this way until she told me that she had an appointment to get an ultrasound. This started me to think something had to be true. This was my first hint of excitement knowing that I was about to see something for the first time that I helped to create after all of these years of uncertainty.

On the day of the ultrasound, we met at the doctor's office and I was still very excited to see my child. As we walked in, I showed no emotion as to how I really felt because there it goes again, that male ego. A short time later we were called into a room to prepare for the ultrasound. As the nurse began the process, I was anxiously waiting to see what was before me. The nurse began by turning a monitor on and putting the jelly on Pepper's stomach. We would be able to see the baby. We looked at the monitor and saw nothing. She soon asked, "Are you sure you're pregnant," Pepper replied "yes." The nurse said "well I see nothing" and turned the machine off. We got up and soon left the office. We were in two separate vehicles and once again I started to wonder, "What is really going on?" This was weighing very heavy on me but of course I didn't show any emotions to Pepper. We went on and our relationship began to move on to the next chapter.

<u>Reality Check:</u> Now the proverbial door slams in my face. After reading how Pepper really felt during this pregnancy, I am literally heart-broken. And yes, she was pregnant and had a miscarriage. I had no idea that she felt the way she did and that I was being such an inconsiderate jackass during all of this. Once I was able to understand how I made her feel, it literally brought me to tears. Seeing things through her eyes, it became clear to me that I showed no concern, no remorse, and no love. After I was able to understand that she felt I didn't care, I fell down to my knees. For the first time, I felt empathy for her. I began to feel a deep sense of remorse for the role I played in adding to her pain. And from a man that feels that he can take almost anything and still stand, I felt extremely little and powerless after this. I talked to Pepper and I believed that I had to apologize repeatedly to show her just how sorry I was. At this point, there was nothing I could do to make any of the past better so I just had to make sure that my actions from this point on were fulfilling an intentional supportive role for her. I have lived from that moment to this one still feeling sorry for my actions and trying to make each and every moment better

for her. This analogy of other side of through gave me a 20/20 hind-sight view. Although we are better now on the other side, I wish that this was one occasion she never had to have gone through alone. Just like I did in this situation, sometimes you don't feel the effects of the storm until after it has passed.

Unfortunately, storms don't come in cute little packages labeled storm 1, storm 2, and storm 3. As described above, one storm may come equipped with several complicated mini-storms all at once. It's time to standstill and stop tip-toeing around the past. It's important to take a look at self, try to realize how the storm arrived, and seek God's help in both exiting the storm and understanding the lessons to be learned.

As previously shared, we experienced two miscarriages. Ironically, there were exactly 9 months to the very day between the two loses. The following is an excerpt from Pepper's journaling of the second miscarriage.

> *1/30/2014*
> *Today I went for my check-up with Dr. Dulaney. Tim and I went into the exam room. "You're growing," she said. All smiles. She put the gooey clear jelly on my belly and pressed the monitor into my stomach. We heard a lot of movement on the sound amplifier but no heartbeat. The doctor kept repositioning the monitor. Then,*

> boom ... boom ... boom. "That is you," she said.
> "That's you all over the place. I will go set up
> the ultra sound." I knew it then, the baby was
> there, with no heartbeat. In the other exam room
> I was told to undress waist down. Next she put
> a clear jelly on my stomach. My uterus was on
> the screen in front of me. "All this black area
> is the amniotic fluid. There is the head and the
> body ... but there is no heartbeat, I'm sorry."
> What my baby is dead?! I heard nothing else.
> The tears began to flow. This can't be true. I've
> already been through this already. But I prayed
> every day. I asked God to protect my baby. Oh,
> Lord. Help me! Dear God what am I going to
> do about Zhariah? She loves this baby with all
> her heart. She will be devastated. Please help.
> Oh Lord send help right away. Good bye my
> precious baby. I will see you in heaven. -Mommy

In life we all are challenged, tried, and tempted time and again. Storms are continuous manifestations of not what is done *to* you, but rather what's being done *for* you. They can be viewed as series of surgeries that are needed to correct life-threatening deficiencies. Like the anguish, stress, and uncertainty of surgery, life storms are painful. In order to get to the other side, we frequently are left with physical, emotional, or psychological scars. But don't be discouraged. Let not your heart be troubled. Be assured, there is help. Pepper suffered through pain and emotional sorrow in the loss of two babies; even so she was never without God's helping hand.

Help is on the way. In order to recognize light at the end of the tunnel of hardship, there are things that you must do. You have to first admit that you need help and be willing to accept help. Next, show your faith by doing your part in actively seeking help from those who are spiritually strong.

It's not about how many times you get knocked down that count; it's how many times you get back up. In order to make sure we are not in a position to get knocked out, we must work hard (have an active role in the Kingdom) and train (study and be actively educated in the Word of God) on a continuous basis. The answers to whatever circumstances or problems that are presented can be found in the Word of God. The Christian existence is not a sprint; rather it is a life-long journey for life-long learners who desire to grow to perfect faith.

You Were Hand Picked

Have your roots planted deep in Christ. Grow in Him. Get your strength from Him. Let Him make you strong in the faith as you have been taught. Your life should be full of thanks to Him.
Colossians 2:7 (NIV)

God has a purpose attached to every problem you face. In all things you are to be thankful. It Isn't always easy to express thankfulness in the midst of difficult times. The key is to focus on where you are going, not where you are. In all circumstances know that it's well with your soul. Why? This storm is only temporary. Like other bad times in your past, it shall also pass. Know that you are normal and your battles are normal. Your same battle has been fought and won by someone else. According to Scripture, no problem is strange or unique; "What has been will be again, what has been done will be done again; there is nothing new under the sun" (Ecclesiastes 1:9 NIV). The disciple Peter also provides assurance that problems are to be expected, "Dear friends, do not be surprised at the fiery ordeal that has come on you to test you, as though something strange were happening to you" (I Peter 4:12 NIV).

Sometimes we have to experience a set-back before the set-up. Remember this is only a temporary set-back that has been purposely assigned to you. No matter how debilitating or frustrating it may be, know that God handpicked you just as He handpicked and favored Job. According to Scripture, Job was "a perfect and an upright man, one that feared God and eschewed evil" (Job 1:8 KJV). You may say, "But I'm not perfect." Are you working towards obedience to God? Do you use your gifts for good and not evil? Do you repent when you go astray? Yes, it's true, *all* have sinned. Yet His desire is that all of His followers seek righteousness. God said, "Be ye therefore perfect, even as your Father which is in heaven is perfect" (Matthew 5:48 KJV). Dear friend, know that perfection is not meant for you to be without sin. It is walking in the way of the Lord, making a habit of choosing good versus evil and you're striving to be without sin.

Perhaps, like Job, God is similarly proud of you and how far you have come in your life. Perhaps He knows how much greater you can be with a little push. Scriptures tell how those who follow Christ will be faced with trials and tribulations (John 16:33 KJV). In his wisdom and understanding of God's power, Job acknowledged his view of the end of his storm; "But he knoweth the way that I take: when he hath tried me, I shall come forth as gold" (Job 23:10 KJV). In order to prepare you for your set-up for success, like gold must be refined and melted, sometimes you will experience the heat of being tried in the fire. The heat is turned up in order to melt you so that you can be molded into something greater. Take a moment and think back on some of the things you used to do that you no longer participate in. Was there a defining moment? Did you experience heat in the form of hardship that prompted the change? Positive change, no matter how big or small is a move toward personal growth.

Storms don't follow textbook pathways. Just like a tornado may enter an area already devastated by war, famine, or a flood, personal storms have no set direction. Even when it seems that we are entering another storm before fully leaving the one we are presently battling, we must remember that God is still there. Often in the heat of the battle, we are left alone to encourage self. Friends, family and loved ones mean well, but may not be able to help in times of need.

How are you to handle life when the bad times come? First, no matter whom you are, how much you have, or how little you have, you are right where you are supposed to be. If it's a troubled mess that you find yourself in, it was chosen for you; but only for a while. In your life you have made many mistakes and experienced adversity of various sorts. Unfortunately, you have many more to come. Even so, it's important to move on.

Better is coming. In order to move forward, first the hurt must be dropped. Stop rehearsing past pain. Stop talking about it, stop thinking about it, and start looking forward to better days. Ask God to show you what you are to learn from past trials. The past is for your learning and the present is a gift. The future is a mystery that you have prepared for by lessons learned from past experiences. There's nothing more beautiful than to pick yourself up with the strength gained from bad times. Encourage yourself by adding a circle of positive people to your world, speak positive words, and think positive thoughts. This renewed disposition inclusive of positive self-talk of God's infinite power adds fuel to your determination to win. A look beyond the present troubles towards victory is important in understanding the power of God. John emphasized individual power to overcome the mountain of trouble simply because you are God's child, he wrote, "Ye are of God, little children, and have overcome them: because greater is he that is in you, than he that is in the world" (I John 4:4 KJV).

A friend once told me that if life was easy, all people would have one. He meant it as a joke; it was funny and sad at the same time because it's true. However, if life is easy and without troubles, then surely the devil is at rest. There is no need to fight hard because you have already been entrapped by his powers. On the other hand, if you win the battle over your adversary, be assured that although he (the devil) will run and leave you alone for a while, he will return (James 4:7 KJV). Getting comfortable in victory is dangerous because the devil does not give up; he has only taken a time-out to regroup. Think of your favorite sports team. When they are playing and ahead by several points over the opposing team, while there is still time left, the opponents take a time out. They go into a huddle to discuss in secret various ways to overpower your favored team. As long as the final bell has not rung, there is still time. As long as there's breathe in a living body, there is still time. There is time to choose God. There is time to actively take your place; time to strive for perfection; time to be the person you were meant to be; and time to make your requests known.

Just Another Storm

He maketh the storm calm, so that the waves thereof are still.
Psalm 107:29 KJV

As a young child, I was significantly afraid of the howling winds and deafening clashes of thunder caused by a severe end-of-season storm. My first instinct was to run and hide. If I had been playing outside, I would immediately run home and go into hiding. Not under the covers, but under the bed. In my mind the covers were not strong enough to keep me safe. I needed something bigger and stronger to protect me. The bed was made of heavy wood and metal to protect me from thunder and lightning that seemingly had a mission to punish me for some slight childish mishap. The ruffled ends of the bed-spread hid my face from the loud wind. As I grew older, I learned to count between clashes of thunder. I knew as the numbers got higher between each bang, that the storm was moving away. Knowing there was an eminent end to the storm, gave me hope.

It took time and maturity for me to learn how to behave in a storm. I stopped running. Instead I rested and waited out the storm. When hell seems to unravel the very essence of life, we must rest and wait it out by turning it all over to

God. Christians must get into habit of standing firm on faith and try God. Let Him handle those problems. He wants to be our refuge just like He did during the tempest storm with the disciples (Matthew 8: 23-27 KJV).

Life is made of three phases: 1) you are headed to a storm, 2) you are in a storm, and 3) you are leaving a storm. This is where the title comes into play, "On the Other Side of Through." This phrase was born when I discovered these three stages of life. Life is made up of several storms that we go through and emerge from.

The first of these phases is **headed to a storm**. In watching the weather channel, the weatherman may say that your area will experience a storm as indicated by the storm-clouds. In life you cannot always tell when you are headed to a storm because the clouds may not always be present. These storms are known as pop-ups. A pop-up storm gives no notice of its arrival, it just happens. These happen in our lives when everything seems to be going well then suddenly, we are hit with a life storm. Consequently, these storms are typically gone as quickly as they arrived.

The next phase is **you are in a storm now**. When in the midst of a storm, it can seem like you have been there for an eternity. Just like any other storm, it only lasts for a short time and then it's gone. When you are in the midst of a storm, it seems like there's nothing you can do to get any comfort or ease from it. No matter how much you pray, cry, plead, or beg, you have to ride the storm out until it's over. These can become some of the most trying times in your life because it forces you to wait until it is over. During the time of our miscarriages we protested, cried, and prayed all while waiting on God to see us through. Waiting causes us to gain patience. The Bible tells us to "let patience have her perfect work, that ye may be perfect and entire, wanting nothing" (James 1: 4 KJV). The purpose of storms like this is to build our patience.

One fact about a storm is no matter how bad, sooner or later it will pass over. The last phase is **just come out of a storm**. When you come out on the other side of a storm, there is much to be thankful and grateful for. It is not always bad to go through a storm because storms teach us lessons along life's journey. If I hadn't gone through storms in life, I wouldn't be the strong person that I am today. Every storm that I have encountered has, in some way or another, affected what and who I am.

While the majority of the population strives to avoid negativity exhibited through chaos, trials, emotional and physical pain, there are others who run to trouble. There are some people who chase storms and there are others who are chased by storms. What's the difference? A storm chaser goes out looking for trouble. Some are thrill seekers. Some have a heroic mentality and try to figure out what caused the storm, and then attempt to place themselves in a position to be viewed as a life-saver. Still others adopt a fanatical mentality by chasing storms to prove their ability to overtake the storm. This makes as much sense as a rabbit attempting to overpower a lion. Though he is smaller and may outsmart the lion in a few battles, ultimately, the lion will win the war. In contrast to the storm chaser are those who seem to have a habit of finding themselves in the midst of trouble because of circumstance and not due to something that they have done or neglected to do. When you get close to God, it may seem that more storms appear. Satan throws his biggest punches when you are right there at the edge of your breakthrough. The reason for this is because your advancement is there on the other side of through when you are in your storm.

At one point in my life I felt enslaved because I was facing issues one after the other with little to no hope of freedom. Although I was going through a lot of mental and emotional anguish, every now and then I did experience a glimpse of relief. Instead of looking at the cons of the storm, I started to focus on the pros. Focusing on the pros taught me that although the storm was raging, it eventually had to end. I realized that I would make it to the other side once I got through the hard times. Through prayer and meditation, I decided to make this revelation a motto to live my life. This motto first became public when I voiced it to my gospel step team one night after practice. As we were about to depart, I told them that I would see them on the other side of through. One of my team members asked, "What does that mean?" I replied, "I don't know what I'm going to go through between

See You On the Other Side of Through

now and when I see you again, but when we do meet again, I will have come through another storm." This phrase stuck with me from that day forward and has become very familiar with my current church family and has been adopted as one of the church's mottos. It has been nearly fifteen years since its origin and it still holds significant value for me and others who learn of the meaning behind the phrase.

It's All Greek to Me

Blessed is he that readeth, and they that hear the words of this prophecy, and keep those things which are written therein: for the time is at hand.
Revelation 1:3 KJV

In chapter one, we talked about the importance of "checking" the mail. Once mail has been checked, reading it is the next step. My mother is a good example of someone who gets bogged down with mail. At any given time a growing mountain of mail can be found somewhere in her home. When asked about it, with a big smile she simply says, "I have to go through all that mail." In protest, I tell her to throw out the junk mail when it arrives, then she wouldn't have such a load. But ignoring my objections, my mother continues to give all mail equal opportunities to take a spot on the mountain of mail. For the purpose of this discussion, authors parallel reading mail with reading the Bible. Many people are overwhelmed with the wording, amount of information, and type of information in the Bible. This can cause frustration that cause some to create excuses for their failure to read the Bible regularly. Others may become so overwhelmed that they refuse to read at all. Our experiences with counseling and teaching has revealed many objections such as: *I would read the Bible more, but I just cannot understand it with all the "thou shalts" and "ye shalls." The Bible was written so long ago, it does not really apply to my life in this day and time. I'm not a strong reader.* Excuses such as these have been used to defend those who may be ill-informed, people pre-occupied with life happenings, those engulfed in a thick fog of selfishness, or those who have a rebellious spirit.

The book of Timothy provides direction for how to be pleasing to the Father, "Study to show thyself approved unto God" (II Timothy 2:15 KJV). During our ministry, we have spoken with countless people who shared their desire to become more knowledgeable, but lacked understanding. There are various translations that help people of various educational levels better understand the Bible. Reading a different version and seeking help from someone you know and trust who is well-versed in the Scriptures could prove to be your best resource when studying.

Understanding may also come by regularly attending congregational meetings, not just attending, but serving as an active participant. Being elderly, young, a woman, new to the congregation, lacking skills in singing, or lacking teaching skills does not provide legitimate excuses for not finding a way to actively participate in serving God. In order to find your way, you may have to try several different ministries before finding the one that best fits your desire, skills, and abilities. I had a fourth grade teacher who loved to tell stories about those who tried and failed versus those who never tried at all. She would quote the well-known anecdote: *If at first you don't succeed try, try again.* Failure is sure to be avoided as long as you never try. If you try and fail, but you learn in the process, that is a sign of personal growth. Continuous growth is demonstrated to God as proof that you are trying.

To get to the other side of a storm, a breakthrough in understanding behavior is needed. Regardless of socioeconomic status, race, ethnicity, sexual orientation, or religious background, basic human needs are food, shelter, clothing, acceptance as a sense of belonging, and intimacy. When addressing acceptance, it is foreseeable that people are attracted to those whom they have shared thoughts, experiences, or beliefs. Ultimately, commonalities may become the breeding ground in which some or all basic needs are met. Hence mini-cultures under the semblance of religious congregations are formed.

Perhaps under conventional orders of leadership, these mini-cultures may aid in the productive nature of the larger realm of society. However, when a collective group places stipulations on its' members regarding acceptable and unacceptable behaviors, the group essentially generates a shared emotional response or group emotional contagion.

For many readers, the above discussion of mini-cultures and church leadership is difficult to understand. Just as there are resources to aid in understanding what is written in the Bible, there is help here. What does this mean? Congregational leadership has the responsibility of helping by providing members with opportunities for learning how to wait with patience for their individual breakthrough. Patience then is defined as how one behaves while waiting. When going through particularly tough situations, it is easy to take on a "woe-is-me" outlook. This is because the view taken is one directly looking at the problem you are currently facing. Although the problem may seem bigger than life, know that it is not. In the famous words of singer/song writer Michael Jackson, "You are not alone." The same thing that you are dealing with right now, others have dealt with and overcome. Just like He was there for others, God is there for you; "Brothers and sisters, as an example of patience in the face of suffering, take the prophets who spoke in the name of the Lord" (James 5:10 KJV). Just like you are suffering in your storms, the prophets also suffered. But God was there for them, and is there today for you.

No matter the severity of the storm, God is in it with you. In the Scriptures, we read that we, being the chosen and dearly loved children of God, have been instructed to add essential characteristics to our personality as individuals who belong to a greater group of believers; "Therefore, as God's chosen people, holy and dearly loved, clothe yourselves with compassion, kindness, humility, gentleness and patience" (Colossians 3:12 KJV). Laziness is not an option. We all have work to do.

Why Does God Hate Me

Unto thee will I cry, O Lord my rock; be not silent to me: lest if thou be silent to me, I become like them that go down into the pit. The Lord is my strength, and he is the saving strength of his anointed.
Psalm 28:1, 8 (KJV)

Every year St. Jude Children's Research Hospital launches massive fundraisers for families affected by pediatric catastrophic diseases. What kind of love is shown when this God we serve allows innocent babies to be born into this world with pain and suffering, having such ailments as cancer and other incurable diseases? How is this fair? How is it justifiable? How could it possibly be Godly? It may not appear to be fair or just. What we have to remember is that God is in control. He wants the best for you even when life is filled with troubles and turmoil. A parent might silently wonder 'why did this have to happen to my child? She is just a baby. Didn't I live a just life? Didn't I give enough money to the church? Didn't I help that family who lost everything in a fire? God, didn't you see me go to church every time the doors opened? Wasn't I the one to always volunteer at the school even though I had no children in attendance? Aren't I a good enough person? THEN WHY MY BABY? Why me? Why my family? Why now?'

When trouble arrives at your front door, it often becomes difficult to hear the voice of God. During these times, feeling His love can be as empty as a song with no sound or a rainbow with no color. If in fact you are His anointed, he has not left you. Be assured, God does not hate you, he loves you and desires that you go to Him with your concerns. Lean on Him. God has abundant strength and enough to take on all cares. While many have held the belief that it is improper, sacrilegious, and even blasphemous to question God, Scripture supports our seeking answers by asking the one who knows all, so ask Him. Ask God those hard questions that bother you at night. Ask Him to show you the answers that no one else has been able to provide. Remember, God is also a parent. Therefore, He understands the pain associated with watching a child, even His only begotten son, suffer unthinkable pain day in and day out. You are His child and He wants to help you.

Why not ask God? Even His only begotten son, Jesus Christ, urges us to ask everything in His name. This is the only way to get the capital t-truth in the answers that you seek (John 18:24 KJV). Perhaps like Rachel you have been faced with a personal illness and feel anxious and a little intimidated about questioning God. Rachel was a fist-year college student away from home for the first time. She had made some good friends, was pledging to become a member of a sorority, had declared physical therapy as her major, was excelling in all classes, and she was living a life-long dream learning how to play the piano. Rachel was excited about how her dreams were coming true. Life for her was wonderful. At the beginning of her second semester in February, she suddenly was stricken with double vision and vertigo. She could not see or walk without assistance. After a series of medical tests finally ending in a painful spinal tap, it was discovered that she had Multiple Sclerosis. Multiple Sclerosis? What is that? Rachel felt all of her dreams and aspirations would now become a vapor in the air. After the doctor explained Multiple Sclerosis was a progressive neurological disease, she became angry with God. "Why me?" Rachel was raised in the church and spent much of her young life witnessing to friends and striving to live righteously. She asked God, why he would allow her to have dreams only to have them crushed by the announcement that she now has an incurable, progressive disease. She wore an eyepatch because of failed vision, and walked with a cane due to extreme complications with balance. With her physical disabilities, Rachel believed her being a physical therapist was out of the question.

Though there were trails of tears and the bitter sting of feeling betrayed, with all her heart and soul, Rachel mustered enough strength to earnestly ask God again, 'Why me?' Almost immediately, the answer that she received was, 'It was going to happen to someone in your family, why not you?' Rachel looked at her mother and father; it could not be either of them, for they were too old and what if it killed them. Her baby sister was too young. Her older sister and brother already had a bus load of physical and personal troubles. Her younger brothers were too immature. Finally, she was able to see that it had to be her burden to bear because she was the only one mature enough and strong enough to handle this new life challenge. Realizing the mercy and glory of God, Rachel began to thank Him. From her hospital bed, she loudly sang songs of praise.

While it is understandable how Rachel could have submerged herself into self-pity, how much more profitable it was for her to look at her situation from another viewpoint. The viewpoint of thankfulness that God spared her family and thankfulness that He had faith in her ability to overcome this obstacle. Life trials often sneak up on us and take us down emotionally-charged pathways. It is normal to feel stressed, sad, angry, and even hopeless. During these times, we must dig down deep within and remember to seek the face of God. Life is full of surprises and disappointments. When you have lemons, don't fret; simply make lemonade. If you have the whole lemon tree; sell the lemons then cut the tree into pieces and sell it for firewood. Basically, make your situation work for you, play the hand that you are dealt. No matter how dim the outlook appears, God never gives us more than we can bare and provides a way out if we look for it. Ask Him to bless you. Perhaps you are not the praying type or you don't know what to say. Try learning the prayer of Jabez. Jabez prayed a simple but effective prayer:

> "Oh, that you would bless me
> and enlarge my territory!
> Let your hand be with me,
> and keep me from harm so that I will be free
> from pain" (I Chronicles 4:10 KJV).

When praying, think of it as a personal conversation with God. There is no need for elaborate words like those sometimes used in public settings by politicians or some well-known preachers. Speak from the heart as Jabez did. He had four requests designed for: 1) God's blessings overall; 2) more financially; 3) God to be by his side; and 4) physical health.

Ask and see how things change in your life. Because we tend to forget, try writing down your requests. Journaling often allows us to see growth in how situations have been handled in the past versus how they are handled today. Often it seems that the answers we seek take so very long. Writing in a journal also serves as a record-keeper of the time it takes God to answer your prayers. Try it; what do you have to lose. You just might be surprised at how fast God actually does answer prayers. Remember, just like any good parent, the answer is not always the one that you want. A good parent will reprimand his child in an effort to save him or her. Spankings hurt; but they are intended to encourage us to change. Some changes require our discontinuing of poor behaviors or feelings. Other chastisements are delivered to compel us to embrace new behaviors. This is why it is vitally important to ask God to be with you and to help guide you regardless of His answer.

Not only can obstacles be overcome, but they can be used to uplift the kingdom and glorify God. Even in the midst of her illness, Rachel felt blessed. She was blessed knowing that God entrusted her with a challenging situation. She was challenged similar to that of Job. Rachel was determined to prove God made a good choice by selecting her. Changing the way we look at life could be the difference in defeat versus triumph by way of additional blessings. The more we are blessed, the more our cup overflows to bless others. Exactly one year after her diagnosis, Rachel returned to the same hospital in the same therapy room. This time it was by choice. While she thought her dreams to become a physical therapist were crushed due to her newly discovered illness, she still pressed forward. After regaining her vision and ability to function independently, she took on a position as a volunteer in the physical therapy department. This time she was the one helping. One of her first and most memorable patients was a college professor who was re-learning how to walk after being stricken with Multiple Sclerosis. Because she made a full recovery from the same illness, she was able to encourage and minister to the professor. Some might say it was ironic. Maybe it was ironic; however, more than irony, it was a true testament to the blessings delivered through God's goodness. Blessings are given based on God's infinite wisdom, grace, mercy, and power. God provides blessing for one simple reason; although sometimes He may hate your actions, He loves you all the time.

Surviving the Storm

Now forgive my sin once more and pray to the Lord your God to take this deadly plague away from me.

Exodus 10:17 NIV

Whether you have been on this life's journey for a long time or for a short while, you have experienced some trying times also known as life's storm. A storm can be simple and complicated at the same time. It is simple in that you know it will come and go, but it is also complicated because you never know what type of storm it will be or how long it is going to last. There are countless types of situations riddled with storms that we are faced with in life that can either make us better or make us bitter.

As a way of coping with trials and tribulations, many talented artists have created musical renditions sharing their stories about personal struggles with various aspects of life. Gospel artists such as Joe Ligon of the Mighty Clouds of Joy sang about fear, hope, and hopelessness during a lengthy period of hardship in the song *I've Been in the Storm too Long*. Another gospel artist, Yolanda Adams, encourages the listener to have both courage and patience while in the midst of difficulties in the song *While Riding Through the Storm*. A storm has no specific area or group that it affects;

we all are at risk of being caught in a down-pour of hardships. You don't have to be religious in order to feel the effects of tornado-like winds of peril or to experience fear associated with standing alone while the ground around you shakes and rumbles in a seemingly never ending tremble. The words of pop singer Amy Winehouse in her song *Rehab* deals with the struggle of facing well-meaning friends and family who insist on addressing personal issues with drugs and alcohol.

As a child you may have been accustomed to running and hiding from a storm. If there is no one to lean on, you encourage yourself. You do not have to hide from the storm, but instead, you can ride out the storm. Riding out the storm shows bravery and strength as you go through. For those who may have been brought up in the church, you may have heard ministers, pastors, church members, and even your parents declare that you just have to pray and have faith. This is easier said than done. It is especially difficult when you don't know how to pray or how to have faith. Country singer Tyler Farr, in his song *Raised to Pray*, speaks about the possibility of escaping the sting of pain and suffering by praying. A prayer is simply a heart-to-heart conversation with a special friend. God is a friend indeed. He is a friend who happens to already know everything that you are dealing with. Still He desires that you tell Him your troubles and that you ask for His help. Faith is the belief that your hopes will come true with no evidence or supporting information.

You see, God specializes in things thought to be impossible and He can do what no other power can. Let us take a brief look into what God has already done. "In the beginning God created the heaven and the earth. The earth was without form and void. Darkness was upon the face of the deep and the spirit of God moved upon the face of the waters" (Genesis 1:1-2 KJV).Then God said, "Let there be light, and there was light. And God said that it was good" (Genesis 1:3 KJV).

In all six days of the creation, God simply said, "Let there be" and whatever he uttered, came to be. Flying things began to fly, creeping things began to creep, swimming things began to swim, hopping things began to hop, crawling things began to crawl and walking things began to walk.

God spoke and light came out of darkness. God spoke and existence came out of nonexistence. God spoke and something came from nothing. If He can simply speak such magnificent things into existence, how much more must He be able to do with changing disorder and chaos to order and organization in your life? Try Him. Try God; what do you have to lose?

Believe and It Shall Be

… Jesus saith unto them, Believe ye that I am able to do this? They said unto him, Yea, Lord. Then touched he their eyes, saying, According to your faith be it unto you.
Matthew 9:28-29 KJV

At 7:28am on Christmas morning, 2015, we welcomed our precious baby girl into our lives. Our God never left us, neither did he forsake us. He prepared us. Sure the pain in losing our previous two babies was great. But God; He knew better. God in His infinite wisdom knew how to allow a series of heart-wrenching incidents to come upon us and then use the experience to be something that was done *for* us. We maintained faith that we would be blessed with a child and God delivered. There is a song that reads, "We will understand it better, by and by." In the by and by, we individually and collectively understand how our past has been able to formulate our present. As long as we kept our eyes on God, He was there to see us through. Times will get hard along the pathway through life (Job 14:1 KJV). But keeping God in plain view will make tough times easier to bear while waiting for the storm to pass.

The following poetic expression speaks to how trials and tribulations are a natural part of life. However, there is hope when trust is placed in God's love and mercy to provide guidance during those times. No one is an expert when handling obstacles, lessons learned through life trials is ongoing.

My life is riddled with hard times and many troubles that I do not understand
But I will keep the faith and believe in my heart it is all part of God's plan
I am learning what is happening is not what is done against, but rather for me
God shows his love and expresses it in ways to guide towards what He would have me to be
If I trust Him, He will be my light in the midst of the storm
He is waiting in anticipation of my renewed self because He trusts my ability to transform
How much stronger, more committed and loving I can become
Through eyes wide shut, walking in blind faith to Him I shall succumb
God used my tribulations to help me and bless others, this I understand and now can see.
Soon this battle will be over, shout "hallelujah" and live eternally!
I am feeling so much joy, I don't know what to do
Thank God in Heaven, I have been so glad since I made it through!

The Rocky Road

Yea, though I walk through the valley of the shadow of death, I will fear no evil: for thou art with me; they rod and thy staff they comfort me.

Psalm 23:4 KJV

One of the most notable limitations of a man is his ability to mask fear and pain all while going about his activities of daily living. Although relatively functional in his pursuit of a normal life, the consistent throbbing of hurt feelings, aching of a broken heart, and the sting of powerlessness when it comes to changing personal situations creates an almost unbearable impression of aloneness. While doing their best to pass through mountains of torture and anguish some men, even some God-fearing men in leadership positions, have fallen into major depression. The only shame is when we, as men, allow our egos to prevent us from seeking help.

Although I am on a level playing ground now, I was once on an obstacle course that seemed to have no end. My journey in life carried me through two failed marriages before I was united with my soul mate. The first of the two was one that I thought would last a lifetime. It started as high school sweethearts, rolled over into college love, and eventually led to marriage. After entering into marriage, I was very happy with Charlote (not her real name). After about two years into the marriage, things took a turn for the worse. I was now not in a happy marriage anymore, however I never showed one ounce of sadness outside of my home. This downhill spiral, which seemed to get worse over time, called for the two of us to eventually get counseling to resolve our issues. Unfortunately, counseling didn't help. Shortly thereafter, I was faced with the statement, "We need a divorce or legal separation." This hit me hard. Driven by my values, I of course agreed to neither because I didn't want to lose my wife; however eventually, we did separate. Charlote and I were apart for only a few months before she began divorce proceedings. When I was presented with divorce papers, it was the worst day of my life. Although we had been separated for some time, I was still in love with her and was experiencing severe heartache. I was able to go through and endure the physical and emotional pain, but it was only the grace of God that kept me.

Between the time of our separation and the beginning of the divorce proceedings, I was called into the ministry to preach God's word. This was a very difficult moment for me because I was still trying to live right while being apart from my wife. The day that I accepted my calling into the ministry, Charlote was out of town, but she was still the person that I called and informed of the news. We were apart, but I felt obligated to her as my wife. Going through this ordeal was dreadful to me because there were some people who said that I only went into the ministry to get my wife back. This was the farthest thing from the truth because I would never say God called me if He didn't just for me to stay with someone. Furthermore, it's very dangerous to play with God like that. Needless to say, the relationship ended, but the ministry continued to thrive.

My journey into the ministry began alone and I preached my first sermon as a single man. I went on preaching and walking this journey for about two years before meeting Diana (not her real name). This young lady eventually became my wife. Our relationship began very abruptly and took off like a flash. Diana and I dated for only about seven months before we were united in marriage. I felt obligated to get married because I was going from place to place preaching God's word, but had no wife. Understanding the culture and popular beliefs of people in areas where I preached, I felt I would be better accepted as a married man. Therefore, being the honorable thing to do in my eyes, Diana and I were united in marriage. Although she was friendly and sweet-tempered, she was still not the right one for me. This relationship lasted about four years before taking a turn for the worse. Due to the severity of the downfall, the marriage eventually ended in divorce. Once this relationship ended, I started to feel like I would never be able to keep any one as my wife. I started to feel less than a preacher, less than a husband, but most of all, I felt less than a man.

I can remember talking to my uncle and telling him, "I'm through with women." He didn't understand what I meant so he asked for clarity. Because I could imagine his concerns for such a statement to come from me, I continued to explain to him what was meant. I was through with women in the sense that I was going to remain single for the rest of my life. This was because I felt like I was a failure. At this point in my life it seemed that everything I touched, failed. All that I was involved in failed. My relationships and even the ministry that I was completely engulfed in was crashing. No matter how much I tried, nothing was working for me.

I began to question God because I thought that either He made a mistake by calling me into the ministry, or maybe I was mistaken in what I heard. Perhaps I thought I heard something that I really didn't hear. I was confused and began questioning myself, my purpose, and I questioned God regarding my very existence. The pain from loss of my relationships, diminished self-worth, and overall disappointment in the path my life had taken was mind boggling. Although people had made negative comments about me some six years earlier, I began to replay those hurtful statements that were made when I accepted the calling into the ministry. At this point in my life, the preaching engagements had decreased, the rumors about me had increased, and my self-esteem had rapidly diminished. Downhearted and hopeless, I felt like a downtrodden nobody. How was I going to be able to tell anyone about the word of God when I couldn't even keep a stable home? The Bible tells us that in order to rule over others, you must first rule your own house well (I Timothy 3:12

KJV). Despite the way I felt and what was still being said about me, I kept going to church every Sunday and Bible study every Wednesday night.

Years later, a church member told me that she watched how I courageously dealt with the negative comments and hurtful accusations of my ex-wife. Because of my actions and continued dedication to God, this lady was able to gain enough courage to handle her own trials. The awesome power of God was used though my pain to uplift someone in their time of need. Sometimes in life, your trials and tribulations are not necessarily limited to lessons for you. During my lowest point, when I thought I was alone, I later learned there were others secretly praying for me and applauding my good-nature. Circumstances negatively affecting you could help someone who may be going through hard times to develop a closer bond with God.

During my alone time after the second divorce, God allowed me to get to know who I really was. The Lord asked, "How can you make someone else happy when you don't know who you are?" The time that God allowed for me to get to know myself was quality time that I needed to spend alone. This time also allowed God to strengthen me in the ministry and confirmed that He really did place a calling on my life and that it was not a mistake. After all was confirmed, my self-esteem began to be reestablished. I lifted my head and once again became proud of the man that I had become. I was appointed to leadership roles in the church, on my job, in the schools, and within the community. God had placed me on a spiral back up the mountain.

During this upward journey, God brought comfort to me by confirming the reason for both of my failed marriages. Scripture states the only reason for divorce according to God is fornication, also defined as sexual immorality (Matthew 5:32; Matthew 19:9; Mark 10:12; I Corinthians 7:10-11 KJV). To my surprise, I was informed by both ex-wives that each ended the marriage because of their own infidelity. After this confirmation, I then knew that both marriages ended with my being in good standing with God. Before I knew the truth, I was very distraught because I had no idea why these relationships were not working out. Additionally, I knew that I could not be married again because "irreconcilable differences" is not Biblically justifiable. After continued prayer and asking God for answers, He confirmed to me just what I needed to start my life over again. With this information, I felt redeemed by God. At last, I was released from mental and emotional torment and could now live my life to the fullest.

In 2009, I ran into someone that I met many years ago while in college. Upon meeting this young lady, I had no idea who she was, but she knew me. While trying to talk to her, she kept drawing back because she said that she already knew of me and my past. Once it was revealed who she was and how we knew each other, I felt that sense of failure once again because she knew of my past failed relationship. I wanted to give up and walk away, but God wouldn't allow me to give up. After our first date, she and I didn't talk or see each other for nine months. Upon reconnecting, we went out and for the first time in a long time, I felt like someone was actually listening to me. I was able to tell my side of my failed marriage and she listened with constructive, yet healing criticism for me.

When God is working things out, Satan is always somewhere trying to tear it back down. Our relationship was going great and we had started to find more and more in common with each other. We both worked, loved God, loved church, and now, we even loved each other. However, there was a dilemma between us, religion. My religious background was Baptist and hers Church of Christ. From past experiences, I knew this would be a major problem for the two of us, but we were dedicated and vowed to work it out. Was it hard? Yes it was hard; however, the love that God put in our hearts for each other helped us to overcome whatever came our way. I knew that I didn't serve a God that would join us together and then allow us to separate because of our religious beliefs. The God that I serve is not a God of confusion.

What God joins to together let no man put asunder (Matthew 19:6 KJV). Three years after meeting the girl of my dreams, I proposed to her one day before she graduated with her doctoral degree. We were engaged for three months before being united in holy matrimony. In my previous marriages, although there were attempts, no children were born. Because I was unsuccessful in producing children with two different women, again I questioned my manhood. Although I wanted and prayed for children in my previous marriages, God said no.

Since being with my soul mate, bone of my bone, flesh of my flesh, I now have one step-daughter, one biological daughter, and a son. I used the term "step-daughter," but she is just as much my daughter as my other two. I love her with all my heart and there is nothing that I wouldn't do for her. This goes to show that sometimes God has to allow us to go the long way around to get where we need to be. What I thought was a "no" from God, was actually "Not now." Not only am I a husband and father, but I am also Pastor of a wonderful congregation of people. If you are wondering what happened with our different religious backgrounds, my wife is now the First Lady of the congregation that I pastor. She is also very active and a leader among the women of this congregation.

If you allow God to take control of your life and follow what He has for you, you will see what He can do for you. I don't know what I'm going to go through between now and the next time you and I meet, but when we see each other again, I will have come through some trials and tribulations and will be on the other side of them. Whether it be sickness, the loss of a loved one, loss of job or possessions, addictions, incarceration or any number of dilemmas that you may face, be assured that you can, with the help of God, get through it. A New Testament writer declared, "We are more than conquerors through Him that loved us" (Romans 8:37 KJV). Not only can you get through your troubles, but you can overcome them. Just hold on.

We have shared stories of how we overcame various life situations along with lessons learned. As stated in the beginning, we all have a story. Those who are financially secure, poor, young, middle-aged, and seniors all have gone through different life trials. You are encouraged to use the pages provided to write your own story and the lessons you learned. Feel free to share your story with us at TLC_Circle@yahoo.com. We will see you on the other side of through.

Scriptural References

Check Your Mail
Psalm 138:7 KJV
Acts 23:16-35 KJV
Luke 6:38 KJV

Delayed, But Not Denied
II Corinthians 4:17 NIV
James 1:19 KJV
Ephesians 4:6 KJV
I Corinthians 13:4, 13 KJV
I Corinthians 16:14 KJV

You Were Handpicked
Colossians 2:7 NIV
Ecclesiastes 1:9 NIV
I Peter 4:12 NIV
Job 1:8 KJV
Matthew 5:48 KJV
John 16:33 KJV
Job 23:10 KJV
I John 4:4 KJV
James 4:7 KJV

Just Another Storm
Psalm 107:29 KJV
Matthew 8: 23-27 KJV
James 1: 4 KJV

It's All Greek To Me
Revelation 1:3 KJV
II Timothy 2:15 KJV
James 5:10 KJV
Colossians 3:12 KJV

Why Does God Hate Me
Psalm 28:1, 8 KJV
John 18:24 KJV
I Chronicles 4:10 KJV

Surviving the Storm
Exodus 10:17 NIV
Genesis 1:1-2 KJV
Genesis 1:3 KJV

Believe and It Shall Be
Matthew 9:28-29 KJV
Job 14:1 KJV

The Rocky Road
Psalm 23:4 KJV
I Timothy 3:12 KJV
Matthew 5:32 KJV
Matthew 19:9 KJV
Mark 10:12 KJV
I Corinthians 7:10-11 KJV
Matthew 19:6 KJV
Romans 8:37 KJV

Printed in the United States
By Bookmasters